The Poetry of Henry Wadsworth Longfellow

Volume IV – The Seaside & the Fireside

Henry Wadsworth Longfellow was born on February 27th, 1807 in Portland, Maine. As a young boy, it was obvious that he was very studious and he quickly became fluent in Latin.

He published his first poem, "The Battle of Lovell's Pond", in the Portland Gazette on November 17th, 1820. He was already thinking of a career in literature and, in his senior year, wrote to his father: "I will not disguise it in the least... the fact is, I most eagerly aspire after future eminence in literature, my whole soul burns most ardently after it, and every earthly thought centers in it...."

After graduation travels in Europe occupied the next three years and he seemed to easily absorb any language he set himself to learn.

On September 14th, 1831, Longfellow married Mary Storer Potter. They settled in Brunswick.

His first published book was in 1833, a translation of poems by the Spanish poet Jorge Manrique. He also published a travel book, Outre-Mer: A Pilgrimage Beyond the Sea.

During a trip to Europe Mary became pregnant. Sadly, in October 1835, she miscarried at some six months. After weeks of illness she died, at the age of 22 on November 29th, 1835. Longfellow wrote "One thought occupies me night and day... She is dead — She is dead! All day I am weary and sad".

In late 1839, Longfellow published Hyperion, a book in prose inspired by his trips abroad.

Ballads and Other Poems was published in 1841 and included "The Village Blacksmith" and "The Wreck of the Hesperus". His reputation as a poet, and a commercial one at that, was set.

On May 10th, 1843, after seven years in pursuit of a chance for new love, Longfellow received word from Fanny Appleton that she agreed to marry him.

On November 1st, 1847, the epic poem Evangeline was published.

In 1854, Longfellow retired from Harvard, to devote himself entirely to writing.

The Song of Haiwatha, perhaps his best known and enjoyed work was published in 1855.

On July 10th, 1861, after suffering horrific burns the previous day. In his attempts to save her Longfellow had also been badly burned and was unable to attend her funeral.

He spent several years translating Dante Alighieri's Divine Comedy. It was published in 1867.

Longfellow was also part of a group who became known as The Fireside Poets which also included William Cullen Bryant, John Greenleaf Whittier, James Russell Lowell, and Oliver Wendell Holmes Snr.

Longfellow was the most popular poet of his day. As a friend once wrote to him, "no other poet was so fully recognized in his lifetime". Some of his works including "Paul Revere's Ride" and "The Song of Haiwatha" may have rewritten the facts but became essential parts of the American psyche and culture.

Henry Wadsworth Longfellow died, surrounded by family, on Friday, March 24th, 1882. He had been suffering from peritonitis.

Index of Contents

THE SEASIDE AND THE FIRESIDE

DEDICATION

As one who, walking in the twilight gloom,
Hears round about him voices as it darkens,
And seeing not the forms from which they come,
Pauses from time to time, and turns and hearkens;

So walking here in twilight, O my friends!
I hear your voices, softened by the distance,
And pause, and turn to listen, as each sends
His words of friendship, comfort, and assistance.

If any thought of mine, or sung or told,
Has ever given delight or consolation,
Ye have repaid me back a thousand-fold,
By every friendly sign and salutation.

Thanks for the sympathies that ye have shown!
Thanks for each kindly word, each silent token,
That teaches me, when seeming most alone,
Friends are around us, though no word be spoken.

Kind messages, that pass from land to land;
Kind letters, that betray the heart's deep history,
In which we feel the pressure of a hand,—
One touch of fire,—and all the rest is mystery!

The pleasant books, that silently among
Our household treasures take familiar places,
And are to us as if a living tongue
Spice from the printed leaves or pictured faces!

Perhaps on earth I never shall behold,
With eye of sense, your outward form and semblance;
Therefore to me ye never will grow old,
But live forever young in my remembrance.

Never grow old, nor change, nor pass away!
Your gentle voices will flow on forever,
When life grows bare and tarnished with decay,
As through a leafless landscape flows a river.

Not chance of birth or place has made us friends,
Being oftentimes of different tongues and nations,
But the endeavor for the selfsame ends,
With the same hopes, and fears, and aspirations.

Therefore I hope to join your seaside walk,
Saddened, and mostly silent, with emotion;
Not interrupting with intrusive talk
The grand, majestic symphonies of ocean.

Therefore I hope, as no unwelcome guest,
At your warm fireside, when the lamps are lighted,
To have my place reserved among the rest,
Nor stand as one unsought and uninvited!

BY THE SEASIDE

THE BUILDING OF THE SHIP

"Build me straight, O worthy Master!
Stanch and strong, a goodly vessel,
That shall laugh at all disaster,
And with wave and whirlwind wrestle!"

The merchant's word
Delighted the Master heard;
For his heart was in his work, and the heart
Giveth grace unto every Art.

A quiet smile played round his lips,
As the eddies and dimples of the tide
Play round the bows of ships,
That steadily at anchor ride.
And with a voice that was full of glee,
He answered, "Erelong we will launch
A vessel as goodly, and strong, and stanch,
As ever weathered a wintry sea!"
And first with nicest skill and art,
Perfect and finished in every part,
A little model the Master wrought,
Which should be to the larger plan
What the child is to the man,
Its counterpart in miniature;
That with a hand more swift and sure
The greater labor might be brought
To answer to his inward thought.

And as he labored, his mind ran o'er
The various ships that were built of yore,
And above them all, and strangest of all
Towered the Great Harry, crank and tall,
Whose picture was hanging on the wall,
With bows and stern raised high in air,
And balconies hanging here and there,
And signal lanterns and flags afloat,
And eight round towers, like those that frown
From some old castle, looking down
Upon the drawbridge and the moat.
And he said with a smile, "Our ship, I wis,
Shall be of another form than this!"
It was of another form, indeed;
Built for freight, and yet for speed,
A beautiful and gallant craft;
Broad in the beam, that the stress of the blast,
Pressing down upon sail and mast,
Might not the sharp bows overwhelm;
Broad in the beam, but sloping aft
With graceful curve and slow degrees,
That she might be docile to the helm,
And that the currents of parted seas,
Closing behind, with mighty force,
Might aid and not impede her course.

In the ship-yard stood the Master,
With the model of the vessel,
That should laugh at all disaster,
And with wave and whirlwind wrestle!

Covering many a rood of ground,
Lay the timber piled around;
Timber of chestnut, and elm, and oak,
And scattered here and there, with these,
The knarred and crooked cedar knees;
Brought from regions far away,
From Pascagoula's sunny bay,
And the banks of the roaring Roanoke!
Ah! what a wondrous thing it is
To note how many wheels of toil
One thought, one word, can set in motion!
There's not a ship that sails the ocean,
But every climate, every soil,
Must bring its tribute, great or small,
And help to build the wooden wall!

The sun was rising o'er the sea,

And long the level shadows lay,
As if they, too, the beams would be
Of some great, airy argosy.
Framed and launched in a single day.
That silent architect, the sun,
Had hewn and laid them every one,
Ere the work of man was yet begun.
Beside the Master, when he spoke,
A youth, against an anchor leaning,
Listened, to catch his slightest meaning.
Only the long waves, as they broke
In ripples on the pebbly beach,
Interrupted the old man's speech.

Beautiful they were, in sooth,
The old man and the fiery youth!
The old man, in whose busy brain
Many a ship that sailed the main
Was modelled o'er and o'er again;—
The fiery youth, who was to be
the heir of his dexterity,
The heir of his house, and his daughter's hand,
When he had built and launched from land
What the elder head had planned.

"Thus," said he, "will we build this ship!
Lay square the blocks upon the slip,
And follow well this plan of mine.
Choose the timbers with greatest care;
Of all that is unsound beware;
For only what is sound and strong
to this vessel stall belong.
Cedar of Maine and Georgia pine
Here together shall combine.
A goodly frame, and a goodly fame,
And the UNION be her name!
For the day that gives her to the sea
Shall give my daughter unto thee!"

The Master's word
Enraptured the young man heard;
And as he turned his face aside,
With a look of joy and a thrill of pride,
Standing before
Her father's door,
He saw the form of his promised bride.
The sun shone on her golden hair,
And her cheek was glowing fresh and fair,

With the breath of morn and the soft sea air.
Like a beauteous barge was she,
Still at rest on the sandy beach,
Just beyond the billow's reach;
But he
Was the restless, seething, stormy sea!
Ah, how skilful grows the hand
That obeyeth Love's command!
It is the heart, and not the brain,
That to the highest doth attain,
And he who followeth Love's behest
Far excelleth all the rest!

Thus with the rising of the sun
Was the noble task begun
And soon throughout the ship-yard's bounds
Were heard the intermingled sounds
Of axes and of mallets, plied
With vigorous arms on every side;
Plied so deftly and so well,
That, ere the shadows of evening fell,
The keel of oak for a noble ship,
Scarfed and bolted, straight and strong
Was lying ready, and stretched along
The blocks, well placed upon the slip.
Happy, thrice happy, every one
Who sees his labor well begun,
And not perplexed and multiplied,
By idly waiting for time and tide!

And when the hot, long day was o'er,
The young man at the Master's door
Sat with the maiden calm and still.
And within the porch, a little more
Removed beyond the evening chill,
The father sat, and told them tales
Of wrecks in the great September gales,
Of pirates coasting the Spanish Main,
And ships that never came back again,
The chance and change of a sailor's life,
Want and plenty, rest and strife,
His roving fancy, like the wind,
That nothing can stay and nothing can bind,
And the magic charm of foreign lands,
With shadows of palms, and shining sands,
Where the tumbling surf,
O'er the coral reefs of Madagascar,
Washes the feet of the swarthy Lascar,

As he lies alone and asleep on the turf.
And the trembling maiden held her breath
At the tales of that awful, pitiless sea,
With all its terror and mystery,
The dim, dark sea, so like unto Death,
That divides and yet unites mankind!
And whenever the old man paused, a gleam
From the bowl of his pipe would awhile illume
The silent group in the twilight gloom,
And thoughtful faces, as in a dream;
And for a moment one might mark
What had been hidden by the dark,
That the head of the maiden lay at rest,
Tenderly, on the young man's breast!

Day by day the vessel grew,
With timbers fashioned strong and true,
Stemson and keelson and sternson-knee,
Till, framed with perfect symmetry,
A skeleton ship rose up to view!
And around the bows and along the side
The heavy hammers and mallets plied,
Till after many a week, at length,
Wonderful for form and strength,
Sublime in its enormous bulk,
Loomed aloft the shadowy hulk!
And around it columns of smoke, up-wreathing.
Rose from the boiling, bubbling, seething
Caldron, that glowed,
And overflowed
With the black tar, heated for the sheathing.
And amid the clamors
Of clattering hammers,
He who listened heard now and then
The song of the Master and his men:—

"Build me straight, O worthy Master.
Stanch and strong, a goodly vessel,
That shall laugh at all disaster,
And with wave and whirlwind wrestle!"

With oaken brace and copper band,
Lay the rudder on the sand,
That, like a thought, should have control
Over the movement of the whole;
And near it the anchor, whose giant hand
Would reach down and grapple with the land,
And immovable and fast

Hold the great ship against the bellowing blast!
And at the bows an image stood,
By a cunning artist carved in wood,
With robes of white, that far behind
Seemed to be fluttering in the wind.
It was not shaped in a classic mould,
Not like a Nymph or Goddess of old,
Or Naiad rising from the water,
But modelled from the Master's daughter!
On many a dreary and misty night,
'T will be seen by the rays of the signal light,
Speeding along through the rain and the dark,
Like a ghost in its snow-white sark,
The pilot of some phantom bark,
Guiding the vessel, in its flight,
By a path none other knows aright!
Behold, at last,
Each tall and tapering mast
Is swung into its place;
Shrouds and stays
Holding it firm and fast!

Long ago,
In the deer-haunted forests of Maine,
When upon mountain and plain
Lay the snow,
They fell,—those lordly pines!
Those grand, majestic pines!
'Mid shouts and cheers
The jaded steers,
Panting beneath the goad,
Dragged down the weary, winding road
Those captive kings so straight and tall,
To be shorn of their streaming hair,
And, naked and bare,
To feel the stress and the strain
Of the wind and the reeling main,
Whose roar
Would remind them forevermore
Of their native forests they should not see again.

And everywhere
The slender, graceful spars
Poise aloft in the air,
And at the mast-head,
White, blue, and red,
A flag unrolls the stripes and stars.
Ah! when the wanderer, lonely, friendless,

In foreign harbors shall behold
That flag unrolled,
'T will be as a friendly hand
Stretched out from his native land,
Filling his heart with memories sweet and endless!

All is finished! and at length
Has come the bridal day
Of beauty and of strength.
To-day the vessel shall be launched!
With fleecy clouds the sky is blanched,
And o'er the bay,
Slowly, in all his splendors dight,
The great sun rises to behold the sight.

The ocean old,
Centuries old,
Strong as youth, and as uncontrolled,
Paces restless to and fro,
Up and down the sands of gold.
His beating heart is not at rest;
And far and wide,
With ceaseless flow,
His beard of snow
Heaves with the heaving of his breast.
He waits impatient for his bride.
There she stands,
With her foot upon the sands,
Decked with flags and streamers gay,
In honor of her marriage day,
Her snow-white signals fluttering, blending,
Round her like a veil descending,
Ready to be
The bride of the gray old sea.

On the deck another bride
Is standing by her lover's side.
Shadows from the flags and shrouds,
Like the shadows cast by clouds,
Broken by many a sunny fleck,
Fall around them on the deck.

The prayer is said,
The service read,
The joyous bridegroom bows his head;
And in tear's the good old Master
Shakes the brown hand of his son,
Kisses his daughter's glowing cheek

In silence, for he cannot speak,
And ever faster
Down his own the tears begin to run.
The worthy pastor—
The shepherd of that wandering flock,
That has the ocean for its wold,
That has the vessel for its fold,
Leaping ever from rock to rock—
Spake, with accents mild and clear,
Words of warning, words of cheer,
But tedious to the bridegroom's ear.
He knew the chart
Of the sailor's heart,
All its pleasures and its griefs,
All its shallows and rocky reefs,
All those secret currents, that flow
With such resistless undertow,
And lift and drift, with terrible force,
The will from its moorings and its course.
Therefore he spake, and thus said he:—
"Like unto ships far off at sea,
Outward or homeward bound, are we.
Before, behind, and all around,
Floats and swings the horizon's bound,
Seems at its distant rim to rise
And climb the crystal wall of the skies,
And then again to turn and sink,
As if we could slide from its outer brink.
Ah! it is not the sea,
It is not the sea that sinks and shelves,
But ourselves
That rock and rise
With endless and uneasy motion,
Now touching the very skies,
Now sinking into the depths of ocean.
Ah! if our souls but poise and swing
Like the compass in its brazen ring,
Ever level and ever true
To the toil and the task we have to do,
We shall sail securely, and safely reach
The Fortunate Isles, on whose shining beach
The sights we see, and the sounds we hear,
Will be those of joy and not of fear!"

Then the Master,
With a gesture of command,
Waved his hand;
And at the word,

Loud and sudden there was heard,
All around them and below,
The sound of hammers, blow on blow,
Knocking away the shores and spurs.
And see! she stirs!
She starts,—she moves,—she seems to feel
The thrill of life along her keel,
And, spurning with her foot the ground,
With one exulting, joyous bound,
She leaps into the ocean's arms!

And lo! from the assembled crowd
There rose a shout, prolonged and loud,
That to the ocean seemed to say,
"Take her, O bridegroom, old and gray,
Take her to thy protecting arms,
With all her youth and all her charms!"

How beautiful she is! How fair
She lies within those arms, that press
Her form with many a soft caress
Of tenderness and watchful care!
Sail forth into the sea, O ship!
Through wind and wave, right onward steer!
The moistened eye, the trembling lip,
Are not the signs of doubt or fear.

Sail forth into the sea of life,
O gentle, loving, trusting wife,
And safe from all adversity
Upon the bosom of that sea
Thy comings and thy goings be!
For gentleness and love and trust
Prevail o'er angry wave and gust;
And in the wreck of noble lives
Something immortal still survives!

Thou, too, sail on, O Ship of State!
Sail on, O UNION, strong and great!
Humanity with all its fears,
With all the hopes of future years,
Is hanging breathless on thy fate!
We know what Master laid thy keel,
What Workmen wrought thy ribs of steel,
Who made each mast, and sail, and rope,
What anvils rang, what hammers beat,
In what a forge and what a heat
Were shaped the anchors of thy hope!

Fear not each sudden sound and shock,
'T is of the wave and not the rock;
'T is but the flapping of the sail,
And not a rent made by the gale!
In spite of rock and tempest's roar,
In spite of false lights on the shore,
Sail on, nor fear to breast the sea
Our hearts, our hopes, are all with thee,
Our hearts, our hopes, our prayers, our tears,
Our faith triumphant o'er our fears,
Are all with thee,—are all with thee!

SEAWEED

When descends on the Atlantic
The gigantic
Storm-wind of the equinox,
Landward in his wrath he scourges
The toiling surges,
Laden with seaweed from the rocks:

From Bermuda's reefs; from edges
Of sunken ledges,
In some far-off, bright Azore;
From Bahama, and the dashing,
Silver-flashing
Surges of San Salvador;

From the tumbling surf, that buries
The Orkneyan skerries,
Answering the hoarse Hebrides;
And from wrecks of ships, and drifting
Spars, uplifting
On the desolate, rainy seas;—

Ever drifting, drifting, drifting
On the shifting
Currents of the restless main;
Till in sheltered coves, and reaches
Of sandy beaches,
All have found repose again.

So when storms of wild emotion
Strike the ocean
Of the poet's soul, erelong
From each cave and rocky fastness,

In its vastness,
Floats some fragment of a song:

Front the far-off isles enchanted,
Heaven has planted
With the golden fruit of Truth;
From the flashing surf, whose vision
Gleams Elysian
In the tropic clime of Youth;

From the strong Will, and the Endeavor
That forever
Wrestle with the tides of Fate
From the wreck of Hopes far-scattered,
Tempest-shattered,
Floating waste and desolate;—

Ever drifting, drifting, drifting
On the shifting
Currents of the restless heart;
Till at length in books recorded,
They, like hoarded
Household words, no more depart.

CHRYSAOR

Just above yon sandy bar,
As the day grows fainter and dimmer,
Lonely and lovely, a single star
Lights the air with a dusky glimmer

Into the ocean faint and far
Falls the trail of its golden splendor,
And the gleam of that single star
Is ever refulgent, soft, and tender.

Chrysaor, rising out of the sea,
Showed thus glorious and thus emulous,
Leaving the arms of Callirrhoe,
Forever tender, soft, and tremulous.

Thus o'er the ocean faint and far
Trailed the gleam of his falchion brightly;
Is it a God, or is it a star
That, entranced, I gaze on nightly!

Ah! what pleasant visions haunt me
As I gaze upon the sea!
All the old romantic legends,
All my dreams, come back to me.

Sails of silk and ropes of sandal,
Such as gleam in ancient lore;
And the singing of the sailors,
And the answer from the shore!

Most of all, the Spanish ballad
Haunts me oft, and tarries long,
Of the noble Count Arnaldos
And the sailor's mystic song.

Like the long waves on a sea-beach,
Where the sand as silver shines,
With a soft, monotonous cadence,
Flow its unrhymed lyric lines:—

Telling how the Count Arnaldos,
With his hawk upon his hand,
Saw a fair and stately galley,
Steering onward to the land;—

How he heard the ancient helmsman
Chant a song so wild and clear,
That the sailing sea-bird slowly
Poised upon the mast to hear,

Till his soul was full of longing,
And he cried, with impulse strong,—
"Helmsman! for the love of heaven,
Teach me, too, that wondrous song!"

"Wouldst thou,"—so the helmsman answered,
"Learn the secret of the sea?
Only those who brave its dangers
Comprehend its mystery!"

In each sail that skims the horizon,
In each landward-blowing breeze,
I behold that stately galley,
Hear those mournful melodies;

Till my soul is full of longing
For the secret of the sea,
And the heart of the great ocean
Sends a thrilling pulse through me.

TWILIGHT

The twilight is sad and cloudy,
The wind blows wild and free,
And like the wings of sea-birds
Flash the white caps of the sea.

But in the fisherman's cottage
There shines a ruddier light,
And a little face at the window
Peers out into the night.

Close, close it is pressed to the window,
As if those childish eyes
Were looking into the darkness,
To see some form arise.

And a woman's waving shadow
Is passing to and fro,
Now rising to the ceiling,
Now bowing and bending low.

What tale do the roaring ocean,
And the night-wind, bleak and wild,
As they beat at the crazy casement,
Tell to that little child?

And why do the roaring ocean,
And the night-wind, wild and bleak,
As they beat at the heart of the mother,
Drive the color from her cheek?

SIR HUMPHREY GILBERT

Southward with fleet of ice
Sailed the corsair Death;
Wild and fast blew the blast,
And the east-wind was his breath.

His lordly ships of ice
Glisten in the sun;
On each side, like pennons wide,
Flashing crystal streamlets run.

His sails of white sea-mist
Dripped with silver rain;
But where he passed there were cast
Leaden shadows o'er the main.

Eastward from Campobello
Sir Humphrey Gilbert sailed;
Three days or more seaward he bore,
Then, alas! the land-wind failed.

Alas! the land-wind failed,
And ice-cold grew the night;
And nevermore, on sea or shore,
Should Sir Humphrey see the light.

He sat upon the deck,
The Book was in his hand
"Do not fear! Heaven is as near,"
He said, "by water as by land!"

In the first watch of the night,
Without a signal's sound,
Out of the sea, mysteriously,
The fleet of Death rose all around.

The moon and the evening star
Were hanging in the shrouds;
Every mast, as it passed,
Seemed to rake the passing clouds.

They grappled with their prize,
At midnight black and cold!
As of a rock was the shock;
Heavily the ground-swell rolled.

Southward through day and dark,
They drift in close embrace,
With mist and rain, o'er the open main;
Yet there seems no change of place.

Southward, forever southward,
They drift through dark and day;

And like a dream, in the Gulf-Stream
Sinking, vanish all away.

THE LIGHTHOUSE

The rocky ledge runs far into the sea,
And on its outer point, some miles away,
The Lighthouse lifts its massive masonry,
A pillar of fire by night, of cloud by day.

Even at this distance I can see the tides,
Upheaving, break unheard along its base,
A speechless wrath, that rises and subsides
In the white lip and tremor of the face.

And as the evening darkens, lo! how bright,
Through the deep purple of the twilight air,
Beams forth the sudden radiance of its light
With strange, unearthly splendor in the glare!

Not one alone; from each projecting cape
And perilous reef along the ocean's verge,
Starts into life a dim, gigantic shape,
Holding its lantern o'er the restless surge.

Like the great giant Christopher it stands
Upon the brink of the tempestuous wave,
Wading far out among the rocks and sands,
The night-o'ertaken mariner to save.

And the great ships sail outward and return,
Bending and bowing o'er the billowy swells,
And ever joyful, as they see it burn,
They wave their silent welcomes and farewells.

They come forth from the darkness, and their sails
Gleam for a moment only in the blaze,
And eager faces, as the light unveils,
Gaze at the tower, and vanish while they gaze.

The mariner remembers when a child,
On his first voyage, he saw it fade and sink;
And when, returning from adventures wild,
He saw it rise again o'er ocean's brink.

Steadfast, serene, immovable, the same

Year after year, through all the silent night
Burns on forevermore that quenchless flame,
Shines on that inextinguishable light!

It sees the ocean to its bosom clasp
The rocks and sea-sand with the kiss of peace;
It sees the wild winds lift it in their grasp,
And hold it up, and shake it like a fleece.

The startled waves leap over it; the storm
Smites it with all the scourges of the rain,
And steadily against its solid form
Press the great shoulders of the hurricane.

The sea-bird wheeling round it, with the din
Of wings and winds and solitary cries,
Blinded and maddened by the light within,
Dashes himself against the glare, and dies.

A new Prometheus, chained upon the rock,
Still grasping in his hand the fire of Jove,
It does not hear the cry, nor heed the shock,
But hails the mariner with words of love.

"Sail on!" it says, "sail on, ye stately ships!
And with your floating bridge the ocean span;
Be mine to guard this light from all eclipse,
Be yours to bring man nearer unto man!"

THE FIRE OF DRIFT-WOOD

DEVEREUX FARM, NEAR MARBLEHEAD

We sat within the farm-house old,
Whose windows, looking o'er the bay,
Gave to the sea-breeze, damp and cold,
An easy entrance, night and day.

Not far away we saw the port,
The strange, old-fashioned, silent town,
The lighthouse, the dismantled fort,
The wooden houses, quaint and brown.

We sat and talked until the night,
Descending, filled the little room;
Our faces faded from the sight,

Our voices only broke the gloom.

We spake of many a vanished scene,
Of what we once had thought and said,
Of what had been, and might have been,
And who was changed, and who was dead;

And all that fills the hearts of friends,
When first they feel, with secret pain,
Their lives thenceforth have separate ends,
And never can be one again;

The first slight swerving of the heart,
That words are powerless to express,
And leave it still unsaid in part,
Or say it in too great excess.

The very tones in which we spake
Had something strange, I could but mark;
The leaves of memory seemed to make
A mournful rustling in the dark.

Oft died the words upon our lips,
As suddenly, from out the fire
Built of the wreck of stranded ships,
The flames would leap and then expire.

And, as their splendor flashed and failed,
We thought of wrecks upon the main,
Of ships dismasted, that were hailed
And sent no answer back again.

The windows, rattling in their frames,
The ocean, roaring up the beach,
The gusty blast, the bickering flames,
All mingled vaguely in our speech.

Until they made themselves a part
Of fancies floating through the brain,
The long-lost ventures of the heart,
That send no answers back again.

O flames that glowed! O hearts that yearned!
They were indeed too much akin,
The drift-wood fire without that burned,
The thoughts that burned and glowed within.

RESIGNATION

There is no flock, however watched and tended,
But one dead lamb is there!
There is no fireside, howsoe'er defended,
But has one vacant chair!

The air is full of farewells to the dying,
And mournings for the dead;
The heart of Rachel, for her children crying,
Will not be comforted!

Let us be patient! These severe afflictions
Not from the ground arise,
But oftentimes celestial benedictions
Assume this dark disguise.

We see but dimly through the mists and vapors;
Amid these earthly damps
What seem to us but sad, funereal tapers
May be heaven's distant lamps.

There is no Death! What seems so is transition;
This life of mortal breath
Is but a suburb of the life elysian,
Whose portal we call Death.

She is not dead,—the child of our affection,—
But gone unto that school
Where she no longer needs our poor protection,
And Christ himself doth rule.

In that great cloister's stillness and seclusion,
By guardian angels led,
Safe from temptation, safe from sin's pollution,
She lives, whom we call dead.

Day after day we think what she is doing
In those bright realms of air;
Year after year, her tender steps pursuing,
Behold her grown more fair.

Thus do we walk with her, and keep unbroken
The bond which nature gives,
Thinking that our remembrance, though unspoken,

May reach her where she lives.

Not as a child shall we again behold her;
For when with raptures wild
In our embraces we again enfold her,
She will not be a child;

But a fair maiden, in her Father's mansion,
Clothed with celestial grace;
And beautiful with all the soul's expansion
Shall we behold her face.

And though at times impetuous with emotion
And anguish long suppressed,
The swelling heart heaves moaning like the ocean,
That cannot be at rest,—

We will be patient, and assuage the feeling
We may not wholly stay;
By silence sanctifying, not concealing,
The grief that must have way.

THE BUILDERS

All are architects of Fate,
Working in these walls of Time;
Some with massive deeds and great,
Some with ornaments of rhyme.

Nothing useless is, or low;
Each thing in its place is best;
And what seems but idle show
Strengthens and supports the rest.

For the structure that we raise,
Time is with materials filled;
Our to-days and yesterdays
Are the blocks with which we build.

Truly shape and fashion these;
Leave no yawning gaps between;
Think not, because no man sees,
Such things will remain unseen.

In the elder days of Art,
Builders wrought with greatest care

Each minute and unseen part;
For the Gods see everywhere.

Let us do our work as well,
Both the unseen and the seen;
Make the house, where Gods may dwell,
Beautiful, entire, and clean.

Else our lives are incomplete,
Standing in these walls of Time,
Broken stairways, where the feet
Stumble as they seek to climb.

Build to-day, then, strong and sure,
With a firm and ample base;
And ascending and secure
Shall to-morrow find its place.

Thus alone can we attain
To those turrets, where the eye
Sees the world as one vast plain,
And one boundless reach of sky.

SAND OF THE DESERT IN AN HOUR-GLASS

A handful of red sand, from the hot clime
Of Arab deserts brought,
Within this glass becomes the spy of Time,
The minister of Thought.

How many weary centuries has it been
About those deserts blown!
How many strange vicissitudes has seen,
How many histories known!

Perhaps the camels of the Ishmaelite
Trampled and passed it o'er,
When into Egypt from the patriarch's sight
His favorite son they bore.

Perhaps the feet of Moses, burnt and bare,
Crushed it beneath their tread;
Or Pharaoh's flashing wheels into the air
Scattered it as they sped;

Or Mary, with the Christ of Nazareth

Held close in her caress,
Whose pilgrimage of hope and love and faith
Illumed the wilderness;

Or anchorites beneath Engaddi's palms
Pacing the Dead Sea beach,
And singing slow their old Armenian psalms
In half-articulate speech;

Or caravans, that from Bassora's gate
With westward steps depart;
Or Mecca's pilgrims, confident of Fate,
And resolute in heart!

These have passed over it, or may have passed!
Now in this crystal tower
Imprisoned by some curious hand at last,
It counts the passing hour,

And as I gaze, these narrow walls expand;
Before my dreamy eye
Stretches the desert with its shifting sand,
Its unimpeded sky.

And borne aloft by the sustaining blast,
This little golden thread
Dilates into a column high and vast,
A form of fear and dread.

And onward, and across the setting sun,
Across the boundless plain,
The column and its broader shadow run,
Till thought pursues in vain.

The vision vanishes! These walls again
Shut out the lurid sun,
Shut out the hot, immeasurable plain;
The half-hour's sand is run!

THE OPEN WINDOW

The old house by the lindens
Stood silent in the shade,
And on the gravelled pathway
The light and shadow played.

I saw the nursery windows
Wide open to the air;
But the faces of the children,
They were no longer there.

The large Newfoundland house-dog
Was standing by the door;
He looked for his little playmates,
Who would return no more.

They walked not under the lindens,
They played not in the hall;
But shadow, and silence, and sadness
Were hanging over all.

The birds sang in the branches,
With sweet, familiar tone;
But the voices of the children
Will be heard in dreams alone!

And the boy that walked beside me,
He could not understand
Why closer in mine, ah! closer,
I pressed his warm, soft hand!

KING WITLAF'S DRINKING-HORN

Witlaf, a king of the Saxons,
Ere yet his last he breathed,
To the merry monks of Croyland
His drinking-horn bequeathed,—

That, whenever they sat at their revels,
And drank from the golden bowl,
They might remember the donor,
And breathe a prayer for his soul.

So sat they once at Christmas,
And bade the goblet pass;
In their beards the red wine glistened
Like dew-drops in the grass.

They drank to the soul of Witlaf,
They drank to Christ the Lord,
And to each of the Twelve Apostles,
Who had preached his holy word.

They drank to the Saints and Martyrs
Of the dismal days of yore,
And as soon as the horn was empty
They remembered one Saint more.

And the reader droned from the pulpit
Like the murmur of many bees,
The legend of good Saint Guthlac,
And Saint Basil's homilies;

Till the great bells of the convent,
From their prison in the tower,
Guthlac and Bartholomaeus,
Proclaimed the midnight hour.

And the Yule-log cracked in the chimney,
And the Abbot bowed his head,
And the flamelets flapped and flickered,
But the Abbot was stark and dead.

Yet still in his pallid fingers
He clutched the golden bowl,
In which, like a pearl dissolving,
Had sunk and dissolved his soul.

But not for this their revels
The jovial monks forbore,
For they cried, "Fill high the goblet!
We must drink to one Saint more!"

GASPAR BECERRA

By his evening fire the artist
Pondered o'er his secret shame;
Baffled, weary, and disheartened,
Still he mused, and dreamed of fame.

'T was an image of the Virgin
That had tasked his utmost skill;
But, alas! his fair ideal
Vanished and escaped him still.

From a distant Eastern island
Had the precious wood been brought
Day and night the anxious master

At his toil untiring wrought;

Till, discouraged and desponding,
Sat he now in shadows deep,
And the day's humiliation
Found oblivion in sleep.

Then a voice cried, "Rise, O master!
From the burning brand of oak
Shape the thought that stirs within thee!"
And the startled artist woke,—

Woke, and from the smoking embers
Seized and quenched the glowing wood;
And therefrom he carved an image,
And he saw that it was good.

O thou sculptor, painter, poet!
Take this lesson to thy heart:
That is best which lieth nearest;
Shape from that thy work of art.

PEGASUS IN POUND

Once into a quiet village,
Without haste and without heed,
In the golden prime of morning,
Strayed the poet's winged steed.

It was Autumn, and incessant
Piped the quails from shocks and sheaves,
And, like living coals, the apples
Burned among the withering leaves.

Loud the clamorous bell was ringing
From its belfry gaunt and grim;
'T was the daily call to labor,
Not a triumph meant for him.

Not the less he saw the landscape,
In its gleaming vapor veiled;
Not the less he breathed the odors
That the dying leaves exhaled.

Thus, upon the village common,
By the school-boys he was found;
And the wise men, in their wisdom,

Put him straightway into pound.

Then the sombre village crier,
Ringing loud his brazen bell,
Wandered down the street proclaiming
There was an estray to sell.

And the curious country people,
Rich and poor, and young and old,
Came in haste to see this wondrous
Winged steed, with mane of gold.

Thus the day passed, and the evening
Fell, with vapors cold and dim;
But it brought no food nor shelter,
Brought no straw nor stall, for him.

Patiently, and still expectant,
Looked he through the wooden bars,
Saw the moon rise o'er the landscape,
Saw the tranquil, patient stars;

Till at length the bell at midnight
Sounded from its dark abode,
And, from out a neighboring farm-yard
Loud the cock Alectryon crowed.

Then, with nostrils wide distended,
Breaking from his iron chain,
And unfolding far his pinions,
To those stars he soared again.

On the morrow, when the village
Woke to all its toil and care,
Lo! the strange steed had departed,
And they knew not when nor where.

But they found, upon the greensward
Where his straggling hoofs had trod,
Pure and bright, a fountain flowing
From the hoof-marks in the sod.

From that hour, the fount unfailing
Gladdens the whole region round,
Strengthening all who drink its waters,
While it soothes them with its sound.

TEGNER'S DRAPA

I heard a voice, that cried,
"Balder the Beautiful
Is dead, is dead!"
And through the misty air
Passed like the mournful cry
Of sunward sailing cranes.

I saw the pallid corpse
Of the dead sun
Borne through the Northern sky.
Blasts from Niffelheim
Lifted the sheeted mists
Around him as he passed.

And the voice forever cried,
"Balder the Beautiful
Is dead, is dead!"
And died away
Through the dreary night,
In accents of despair.

Balder the Beautiful,
God of the summer sun,
Fairest of all the Gods!
Light from his forehead beamed,
Runes were upon his tongue,
As on the warrior's sword.

All things in earth and air
Bound were by magic spell
Never to do him harm;
Even the plants and stones;
All save the mistletoe,
The sacred mistletoe!

Hoeder, the blind old God,
Whose feet are shod with silence,
Pierced through that gentle breast
With his sharp spear, by fraud
Made of the mistletoe,
The accursed mistletoe!

They laid him in his ship,
With horse and harness,
As on a funeral pyre.

Odin placed
A ring upon his finger,
And whispered in his ear.

They launched the burning ship!
It floated far away
Over the misty sea,
Till like the sun it seemed,
Sinking beneath the waves.
Balder returned no more!

So perish the old Gods!
But out of the sea of Time
Rises a new land of song,
Fairer than the old.
Over its meadows green
Walk the young bards and sing.

Build it again,
O ye bards,
Fairer than before!
Ye fathers of the new race,
Feed upon morning dew,
Sing the new Song of Love!

The law of force is dead!
The law of love prevails!
Thor, the thunderer,
Shall rule the earth no more,
No more, with threats,
Challenge the meek Christ.

Sing no more,
O ye bards of the North,
Of Vikings and of Jarls!
Of the days of Eld
Preserve the freedom only,
Not the deeds of blood!

SONNET

ON MRS. KEMBLE'S READINGS FROM SHAKESPEARE

O precious evenings! all too swiftly sped!
Leaving us heirs to amplest heritages
Of all the best thoughts of the greatest sages,

And giving tongues unto the silent dead!
How our hearts glowed and trembled as she read,
Interpreting by tones the wondrous pages
Of the great poet who foreruns the ages,
Anticipating all that shall be said!
O happy Reader! having for thy text
The magic book, whose Sibylline leaves have caught
The rarest essence of all human thought!
O happy Poet! by no critic vext!
How must thy listening spirit now rejoice
To be interpreted by such a voice!

THE SINGERS

God sent his Singers upon earth
With songs of sadness and of mirth,
That they might touch the hearts of men,
And bring them back to heaven again.

The first, a youth, with soul of fire,
Held in his hand a golden lyre;
Through groves he wandered, and by streams,
Playing the music of our dreams.

The second, with a bearded face,
Stood singing in the market-place,
And stirred with accents deep and loud
The hearts of all the listening crowd.

A gray old man, the third and last,
Sang in cathedrals dim and vast,
While the majestic organ rolled
Contrition from its mouths of gold.

And those who heard the Singers three
Disputed which the best might be;
For still their music seemed to start
Discordant echoes in each heart,

But the great Master said, "I see
No best in kind, but in degree;
I gave a various gift to each,
To charm, to strengthen, and to teach.

"These are the three great chords of might,
And he whose ear is tuned aright

Will hear no discord in the three,
But the most perfect harmony."

SUSPIRIA

Take them, O Death! and bear away
Whatever thou canst call thine own!
Thine image, stamped upon this clay,
Doth give thee that, but that alone!

Take them, O Grave! and let them lie
Folded upon thy narrow shelves,
As garments by the soul laid by,
And precious only to ourselves!

Take them, O great Eternity!
Our little life is but a gust
That bends the branches of thy tree,
And trails its blossoms in the dust!

HYMN

FOR MY BROTHER'S ORDINATION

Christ to the young man said: "Yet one thing more;
If thou wouldst perfect be,
Sell all thou hast and give it to the poor,
And come and follow me!"

Within this temple Christ again, unseen,
Those sacred words hath said,
And his invisible hands to-day have been
Laid on a young man's head.

And evermore beside him on his way
The unseen Christ shall move,
That he may lean upon his arm and say,
"Dost thou, dear Lord, approve?"

Beside him at the marriage feast shall be,
To make the scene more fair;
Beside him in the dark Gethsemane
Of pain and midnight prayer.

O holy trust! O endless sense of rest!
Like the beloved John
To lay his head upon the Saviour's breast,
And thus to journey on!

FLOWER-DE-LUCE

FLOWER-DE-LUCE

Beautiful lily, dwelling by still rivers,
Or solitary mere,
Or where the sluggish meadow-brook delivers
Its waters to the weir!

Thou laughest at the mill, the whir and worry
Of spindle and of loom,
And the great wheel that toils amid the hurry
And rushing of the flame.

Born in the purple, born to joy and pleasance,
Thou dost not toil nor spin,
But makest glad and radiant with thy presence
The meadow and the lin.

The wind blows, and uplifts thy drooping banner,
And round thee throng and run
The rushes, the green yeomen of thy manor,
The outlaws of the sun.

The burnished dragon-fly is thine attendant,
And tilts against the field,
And down the listed sunbeam rides resplendent
With steel-blue mail and shield.

Thou art the Iris, fair among the fairest,
Who, armed with golden rod
And winged with the celestial azure, bearest
The message of some God.

Thou art the Muse, who far from crowded cities
Hauntest the sylvan streams,
Playing on pipes of reed the artless ditties
That come to us as dreams.

O flower-de-luce, bloom on, and let the river
Linger to kiss thy feet!

O flower of song, bloom on, and make forever
The world more fair and sweet.

PALINGENESIS

I lay upon the headland-height, and listened
To the incessant sobbing of the sea
In caverns under me,
And watched the waves, that tossed and fled and glistened,
Until the rolling meadows of amethyst
Melted away in mist.

Then suddenly, as one from sleep, I started;
For round about me all the sunny capes
Seemed peopled with the shapes
Of those whom I had known in days departed,
Apparelled in the loveliness which gleams
On faces seen in dreams.

A moment only, and the light and glory
Faded away, and the disconsolate shore
Stood lonely as before;
And the wild-roses of the promontory
Around me shuddered in the wind, and shed
Their petals of pale red.

There was an old belief that in the embers
Of all things their primordial form exists,
And cunning alchemists
Could re-create the rose with all its members
From its own ashes, but without the bloom,
Without the lost perfume.

Ah me! what wonder-working, occult science
Can from the ashes in our hearts once more
The rose of youth restore?
What craft of alchemy can bid defiance
To time and change, and for a single hour
Renew this phantom-flower?

"O, give me back," I cried, "the vanished splendors,
The breath of morn, and the exultant strife,
When the swift stream of life
Bounds o'er its rocky channel, and surrenders
The pond, with all its lilies, for the leap
Into the unknown deep!"

And the sea answered, with a lamentation,
Like some old prophet wailing, and it said,
"Alas! thy youth is dead!
It breathes no more, its heart has no pulsation;
In the dark places with the dead of old
It lies forever cold!"

Then said I, "From its consecrated cerements
I will not drag this sacred dust again,
Only to give me pain;
But, still remembering all the lost endearments,
Go on my way, like one who looks before,
And turns to weep no more."

Into what land of harvests, what plantations
Bright with autumnal foliage and the glow
Of sunsets burning low;
Beneath what midnight skies, whose constellations
Light up the spacious avenues between
This world and the unseen!

Amid what friendly greetings and caresses,
What households, though not alien, yet not mine,
What bowers of rest divine;
To what temptations in lone wildernesses,
What famine of the heart, what pain and loss,
The bearing of what cross!

I do not know; nor will I vainly question
Those pages of the mystic book which hold
The story still untold,
But without rash conjecture or suggestion
Turn its last leaves in reverence and good heed,
Until "The End" I read.

THE BRIDGE OF CLOUD

Burn, O evening hearth, and waken
Pleasant visions, as of old!
Though the house by winds be shaken,
Safe I keep this room of gold!

Ah, no longer wizard Fancy
Builds her castles in the air,
Luring me by necromancy

Up the never-ending stair!

But, instead, she builds me bridges
Over many a dark ravine,
Where beneath the gusty ridges
Cataracts dash and roar unseen.

And I cross them, little heeding
Blast of wind or torrent's roar,
As I follow the receding
Footsteps that have gone before.

Naught avails the imploring gesture,
Naught avails the cry of pain!
When I touch the flying vesture,
'T is the gray robe of the rain.

Baffled I return, and, leaning
O'er the parapets of cloud,
Watch the mist that intervening
Wraps the valley in its shroud.

And the sounds of life ascending
Faintly, vaguely, meet the ear,
Murmur of bells and voices blending
With the rush of waters near.

Well I know what there lies hidden,
Every tower and town and farm,
And again the land forbidden
Reassumes its vanished charm.

Well I know the secret places,
And the nests in hedge and tree;
At what doors are friendly faces,
In what hearts are thoughts of me.

Through the mist and darkness sinking,
Blown by wind and beaten by shower,
Down I fling the thought I'm thinking,
Down I toss this Alpine flower.

HAWTHORNE

MAY 23, 1864

How beautiful it was, that one bright day
In the long week of rain!
Though all its splendor could not chase away
The omnipresent pain.

The lovely town was white with apple-blooms,
And the great elms o'erhead
Dark shadows wove on their aerial looms
Shot through with golden thread.

Across the meadows, by the gray old manse,
The historic river flowed:
I was as one who wanders in a trance,
Unconscious of his road.

The faces of familiar friends seemed strange;
Their voices I could hear,
And yet the words they uttered seemed to change
Their meaning to my ear.

For the one face I looked for was not there,
The one low voice was mute;
Only an unseen presence filled the air,
And baffled my pursuit.

Now I look back, and meadow, manse, and stream
Dimly my thought defines;
I only see—a dream within a dream—
The hill-top hearsed with pines.

I only hear above his place of rest
Their tender undertone,
The infinite longings of a troubled breast,
The voice so like his own.

There in seclusion and remote from men
The wizard hand lies cold,
Which at its topmost speed let fall the pen,
And left the tale half told.

Ah! who shall lift that wand of magic power,
And the lost clew regain?
The unfinished window in Aladdin's tower
Unfinished must remain!

CHRISTMAS BELLS

I heard the bells on Christmas Day
Their old, familiar carols play,
And wild and sweet
The words repeat
Of peace on earth, good-will to men!

And thought how, as the day had come,
The belfries of all Christendom
Had rolled along
The unbroken song
Of peace on earth, good-will to men!

Till, ringing, singing on its way,
The world revolved from night to day,
A voice, a chime,
A chant sublime
Of peace on earth, good-will to men!

Then from each black, accursed mouth
The cannon thundered in the South,
And with the sound
The carols drowned
Of peace on earth, good-will to men!

It was as if an earthquake rent
The hearth-stones of a continent,
And made forlorn
The households born
Of peace on earth, good-will to men!

And in despair I bowed my head;
"There is no peace on earth," I said:
"For hate is strong,
And mocks the song
Of peace on earth, good-will to men!"

Then pealed the bells more loud and deep:
"God is not dead; nor doth he sleep!
The Wrong shall fail,
The Right prevail,
With peace on earth, good-will to men!"

THE WIND OVER THE CHIMNEY

See, the fire is sinking low,

Dusky red the embers glow,
While above them still I cower,
While a moment more I linger,
Though the clock, with lifted finger,
Points beyond the midnight hour.

Sings the blackened log a tune
Learned in some forgotten June
From a school-boy at his play,
When they both were young together,
Heart of youth and summer weather
Making all their holiday.

And the night-wind rising, hark!
How above there in the dark,
In the midnight and the snow,
Ever wilder, fiercer, grander,
Like the trumpets of Iskander,
All the noisy chimneys blow!

Every quivering tongue of flame
Seems to murmur some great name,
Seems to say to me, "Aspire!"
But the night-wind answers, "Hollow
Are the visions that you follow,
Into darkness sinks your fire!"

Then the flicker of the blaze
Gleams on volumes of old days,
Written by masters of the art,
Loud through whose majestic pages
Rolls the melody of ages,
Throb the harp-strings of the heart.

And again the tongues of flame
Start exulting and exclaim:
"These are prophets, bards, and seers;
In the horoscope of nations,
Like ascendant constellations,
They control the coming years."

But the night-wind cries: "Despair!
Those who walk with feet of air
Leave no long-enduring marks;
At God's forges incandescent
Mighty hammers beat incessant,
These are but the flying sparks.

"Dust are all the hands that wrought;
Books are sepulchres of thought;
The dead laurels of the dead
Rustle for a moment only,
Like the withered leaves in lonely
Churchyards at some passing tread."

Suddenly the flame sinks down;
Sink the rumors of renown;
And alone the night-wind drear
Clamors louder, wilder, vaguer,—
"'T is the brand of Meleager
Dying on the hearth-stone here!"

And I answer,—"Though it be,
Why should that discomfort me?
No endeavor is in vain;
Its reward is in the doing,
And the rapture of pursuing
Is the prize the vanquished gain."

THE BELLS OF LYNN

HEARD AT NAHANT

O curfew of the setting sun! O Bells of Lynn!
O requiem of the dying day! O Bells of Lynn!

From the dark belfries of yon cloud-cathedral wafted,
Your sounds aerial seem to float, O Bells of Lynn!

Borne on the evening wind across the crimson twilight,
O'er land and sea they rise and fall, O Bells of Lynn!

The fisherman in his boat, far out beyond the headland,
Listens, and leisurely rows ashore, O Bells of Lynn!

Over the shining sands the wandering cattle homeward
Follow each other at your call, O Bells of Lynn!

The distant lighthouse hears, and with his flaming signal
Answers you, passing the watchword on, O Bells of Lynn!

And down the darkening coast run the tumultuous surges,
And clap their hands, and shout to you, O Bells of Lynn!

Till from the shuddering sea, with your wild incantations,
Ye summon up the spectral moon, O Bells of Lynn!

And startled at the sight like the weird woman of Endor,
Ye cry aloud, and then are still, O Bells of Lynn!

KILLED AT THE FORD

He is dead, the beautiful youth,
The heart of honor, the tongue of truth,
He, the life and light of us all,
Whose voice was blithe as a bugle-call,
Whom all eyes followed with one consent,
The cheer of whose laugh, and whose pleasant word,
Hushed all murmurs of discontent.

Only last night, as we rode along,
Down the dark of the mountain gap,
To visit the picket-guard at the ford,
Little dreaming of any mishap,
He was humming the words of some old song:
"Two red roses he had on his cap,
And another he bore at the point of his sword."

Sudden and swift a whistling ball
Came out of a wood, and the voice was still;
Something I heard in the darkness fall,
And for a moment my blood grew chill;
I spake in a whisper, as he who speaks
In a room where some one is lying dead;
But he made no answer to what I said.

We lifted him up to his saddle again,
And through the mire and the mist and the rain
Carried him back to the silent camp,
And laid him as if asleep on his bed;
And I saw by the light of the surgeon's lamp
Two white roses upon his cheeks,
And one, just over his heart, blood-red!

And I saw in a vision how far and fleet
That fatal bullet went speeding forth,
Till it reached a town in the distant North,
Till it reached a house in a sunny street,
Till it reached a heart that ceased to beat
Without a murmur, without a cry;

And a bell was tolled, in that far-off town,
For one who had passed from cross to crown,
And the neighbors wondered that she should die.

GIOTTO'S TOWER

How many lives, made beautiful and sweet
By self-devotion and by self-restraint,
Whose pleasure is to run without complaint
On unknown errands of the Paraclete,
Wanting the reverence of unshodden feet,
Fail of the nimbus which the artists paint
Around the shining forehead of the saint,
And are in their completeness incomplete!
In the old Tuscan town stands Giotto's tower,
The lily of Florence blossoming in stone,—
A vision, a delight, and a desire,—
The builder's perfect and centennial flower,
That in the night of ages bloomed alone,
But wanting still the glory of the spire.

TO-MORROW

'T is late at night, and in the realm of sleep
My little lambs are folded like the flocks;
From room to room I hear the wakeful clocks
Challenge the passing hour, like guards that keep
Their solitary watch on tower and steep;
Far off I hear the crowing of the cocks,
And through the opening door that time unlocks
Feel the fresh breathing of To-morrow creep.
To-morrow! the mysterious, unknown guest,
Who cries to me: "Remember Barmecide,
And tremble to be happy with the rest."
And I make answer: "I am satisfied;
I dare not ask; I know not what is best;
God hath already said what shall betide."

DIVINA COMMEDIA

I

Oft have I seen at some cathedral door
A laborer, pausing in the dust and heat,
Lay down his burden, and with reverent feet
Enter, and cross himself, and on the floor
Kneel to repeat his paternoster o'er;
Far off the noises of the world retreat;
The loud vociferations of the street
Become an undistinguishable roar.
So, as I enter here from day to day,
And leave my burden at this minster gate,
Kneeling in prayer, and not ashamed to pray,
The tumult of the time disconsolate
To inarticulate murmurs dies away,
While the eternal ages watch and wait.

II

How strange the sculptures that adorn these towers!
This crowd of statues, in whose folded sleeves
Birds build their nests; while canopied with leaves
Parvis and portal bloom like trellised bowers,
And the vast minster seems a cross of flowers!
But fiends and dragons on the gargoyled eaves
Watch the dead Christ between the living thieves,
And, underneath, the traitor Judas lowers!
Ah! from what agonies of heart and brain,
What exultations trampling on despair,
What tenderness, what tears, what hate of wrong,
What passionate outcry of a soul in pain,
Uprose this poem of the earth and air,
This medieval miracle of song!

III

I enter, and I see thee in the gloom
Of the long aisles, O poet saturnine!
And strive to make my steps keep pace with thine.
The air is filled with some unknown perfume;
The congregation of the dead make room
For thee to pass; the votive tapers shine;
Like rooks that haunt Ravenna's groves of pine
The hovering echoes fly from tomb to tomb.
From the confessionals I hear arise
Rehearsals of forgotten tragedies,
And lamentations from the crypts below;
And then a voice celestial, that begins

With the pathetic words, "Although your sins
As scarlet be," and ends with "as the snow."

IV

With snow-white veil and garments as of flame,
She stands before thee, who so long ago
Filled thy young heart with passion and the woe
From which thy song and all its splendors came;
And while with stern rebuke she speaks thy name,
The ice about thy heart melts as the snow
On mountain height; and in swift overflow
Comes gushing from thy lips in sobs of shame.
Thou makest full confession; and a gleam,
As of the dawn on some dark forest cast,
Seems on thy lifted forehead to increase;
Lethe and Eunoe—the remembered dream
And the forgotten sorrow—bring at last
That perfect pardon which is perfect peace.

V

I lift mine eyes, and all the windows blaze
With forms of saints and holy men who died,
Here martyred and hereafter glorified;
And the great Rose upon its leaves displays
Christ's Triumph, and the angelic roundelays,
With splendor upon splendor multiplied;
And Beatrice again at Dante's side
No more rebukes, but smiles her words of praise.
And then the organ sounds, and unseen choirs
Sing the old Latin hymns of peace and love,
And benedictions of the Holy Ghost;
And the melodious bells among the spires
O'er all the house-tops and through heaven above
Proclaim the elevation of the Host!

VI

O star of morning and of liberty!
O bringer of the light, whose splendor shines
Above the darkness of the Apennines,
Forerunner of the day that is to be!
The voices of the city and the sea,
The voices of the mountains and the pines,

Repeat thy song, till the familiar lines
Are footpaths for the thought of Italy!
Thy fame is blown abroad from all the heights,
Through all the nations, and a sound is heard,
As of a mighty wind, and men devout,
Strangers of Rome, and the new proselytes,
In their own language hear thy wondrous word,
And many are amazed and many doubt.

NOEL

ENVOYE A M. AGASSIZ, LA VEILLE DE NOEL 1864, AVEC UN PANIER DE VINS DIVERS

L'Academie en respect,
Nonobstant l'incorrection
A la faveur du sujet,
Ture-lure,
N'y fera point de rature;
Noel! ture-lure-lure.
— Gui Barozai

Quand les astres de Noel
Brillaient, palpitaient au ciel,
Six gaillards, et chacun ivre,
Chantaient gaiment dans le givre,
"Bons amis,
Allons donc chez Agassiz!"

Ces illustres Pelerins
D'Outre-Mer adroits et fins,
Se donnant des airs de pretre,
A l'envi se vantaient d'etre
"Bons amis,
De Jean Rudolphe Agassiz!"

Oeil-de-Perdrix, grand farceur,
Sans reproche et sans pudeur,
Dans son patois de Bourgogne,
Bredouillait comme un ivrogne,
"Bons amis,
J'ai danse chez Agassiz!"

Verzenay le Champenois,
Bon Francais, point New-Yorquois,
Mais des environs d'Avize,
Fredonne a mainte reprise,

"Bons amis,
J'ai chante chez Agassiz!"

A cote marchait un vieux
Hidalgo, mais non mousseux;
Dans le temps de Charlemagne
Fut son pere Grand d'Espagne!
"Bons amis,
J'ai dine chez Agassiz!"

Derriere eux un Bordelais,
Gascon, s'il en fut jamais,
Parfume de poesie
Riait, chantait, plein de vie,
"Bons amis,
J'ai soupe chez Agassiz!"

Avec ce beau cadet roux,
Bras dessus et bras dessous,
Mine altiere et couleur terne,
Vint le Sire de Sauterne;
"Bons amis,
J'ai couche chez Agassiz!"

Mais le dernier de ces preux,
Etait un pauvre Chartreux,
Qui disait, d'un ton robuste,
"Benedictions sur le Juste!
Bons amis,
Benissons Pere Agassiz!"

Ils arrivent trois a trois,
Montent l'escalier de bois
Clopin-clopant! quel gendarme
Peut permettre ce vacarme,
Bons amis,
A la porte d'Agassiz!

"Ouvrer donc, mon bon Seigneur,
Ouvrez vite et n'ayez peur;
Ouvrez, ouvrez, car nous sommes
Gens de bien et gentilshommes,
Bons amis
De la famille Agassiz!"

Chut, ganaches! taisez-vous!
C'en est trop de vos glouglous;
Epargnez aux Philosophes

Vos abominables strophes!
Bons amis,
Respectez mon Agassiz!

Henry Wadsworth Longfellow – A Short Biography

Henry Wadsworth Longfellow was born on February 27th, 1807 in Portland, Maine (then part of Massachusetts) to Stephen Longfellow and Zilpah (nee Wadsworth) Longfellow. His father was a lawyer, and his maternal grandfather, Peleg Wadsworth, was a general in the American Revolutionary War and a Member of Congress.

It was a large family. Longfellow was the second of eight children; his siblings were Stephen (1805), Elizabeth (1808), Anne (1810), Alexander (1814), Mary (1816), Ellen (1818) and Samuel (1819).

Longfellow attended a dame school at the age of three and by age six was enrolled at the private Portland Academy. He was very studious and quickly became fluent in Latin. His mother encouraged his love of reading and learning and introduced him to many literary classics.

He published his first poem, a patriotic four-stanza affair entitled "The Battle of Lovell's Pond", in the Portland Gazette on November 17, 1820. He remained at the Portland Academy until he was fourteen. As a child, he spent much of his summers at his grandfather Peleg's farm in the nearby town of Hiram.

In the fall of 1822, the 15-year-old Longfellow enrolled at Bowdoin College in Brunswick, Maine. His grandfather was a founder of the college and his father a trustee. Here he met and befriended Nathaniel Hawthorne. Longfellow was already thinking of a career in literature. In his senior year he wrote to his father: "I will not disguise it in the least... the fact is, I most eagerly aspire after future eminence in literature, my whole soul burns most ardently after it, and every earthly thought centers in it... I am almost confident in believing, that if I can ever rise in the world it must be by the exercise of my talents in the wide field of literature."

Poetry was the writing form he felt most at ease with and he offered poems to many newspapers and magazines. Between January 1824 and graduation in 1825, he had almost 40 poems published, over half of which were in the short-lived Boston periodical The United States Literary Gazette.

When Longfellow graduated, he was ranked a pleasing fourth in the class, and had been elected to Phi Beta Kappa. He was quickly offered the post of professor of modern languages at his alma mater.

Accounts suggest that part of the requirement of acceptance was to tour Europe to become more immersed in both languages and cultures. Longfellow began his tour of Europe in May 1826 aboard the ship Cadmus. His travels in Europe would last three years and cost his father the princely sum of $2,604.24. He visited France, Spain, Italy, Germany and England before returning to the United States in mid-August 1829.

His stock of languages now included French, Spanish, Portuguese, and German, and impressively, mostly without any formal instruction.

On August 27th, 1829, he wrote to the president of Bowdoin that he was turning down the professorship because he considered the $600 salary "disproportionate to the duties required". The trustees countered by raising the salary to $800 and an additional $100 to serve as the college's librarian, a post which required only one hour's attention a day.

On September 14th, 1831, Longfellow married Mary Storer Potter, a childhood friend from Portland. The couple settled in Brunswick. Longfellow now published several non-fiction and fiction prose pieces inspired by his friend Washington Irving, whom he had met in Madrid during his travels, these included "The Indian Summer" and "The Bald Eagle" in 1833.

During his years teaching at the college, he translated textbooks in French, Italian and Spanish; his first published book was in 1833, a translation of the poetry of the medieval Spanish poet Jorge Manrique. A travel book, Outre-Mer: A Pilgrimage Beyond the Sea, was first published in serial form before a book edition in 1835.

In December 1834, Longfellow received a letter from Josiah Quincy III, president of Harvard College, offering him the Smith Professorship of Modern Languages with the condition that he first spend a year or so abroad. The Longfellow's set off for Europe. He would now be able to add German, Dutch, Danish, Swedish, Finnish, and Icelandic to his repertoire of languages.

During the trip they discovered that Mary was pregnant. Sadly, in October 1835, she miscarried some six months into the pregnancy. Then followed several weeks of illness and at the age of 22 on November 29th, 1835 she died. Longfellow had her body embalmed, placed in a lead coffin itself inside an oak coffin which was then shipped to Mount Auburn Cemetery near Boston. He wrote movingly "One thought occupies me night and day... She is dead—She is dead! All day I am weary and sad".

Back in the United States, Longfellow took up the professorship at Harvard. He was required to live in Cambridge, close to the campus and rented rooms at the Craigie House in the spring of 1837. The home, built in 1759, had once been the headquarters of George Washington during the Siege of Boston.

Longfellow now felt able to publish again, starting with the collection Voices of the Night in 1839. It was mainly comprised of translations together with nine original poems and seven poems written back in his teenage years.

His romantic interests also began to surface again. He had begun to court Frances 'Fanny' Appleton, daughter of the Boston industrialist Nathan Appleton. At first, the independent-minded Appleton was not interested in marriage but Longfellow was determined. In July 1839, he wrote to a friend: "Victory hangs doubtful. The lady says she will not! I say she shall! It is not pride, but the madness of passion".

In late 1839, Longfellow published Hyperion, a book in prose inspired by his trips abroad and his still unsuccessful courtship of Fanny Appleton. Amidst this, Longfellow fell into "periods of neurotic depression with moments of panic" and required a six-month leave of absence from Harvard to attend a health spa in the former Marienberg Benedictine Convent at Boppard in Germany.

Ballads and Other Poems was published in 1841 and included "The Village Blacksmith" and "The Wreck of the Hesperus". His reputation as a poet, and a commercial one at that, was set.

Longfellow published a play in 1842, The Spanish Student, based on his memories from his time in Spain in the 1820s. A small collection, Poems on Slavery, was also published in 1842. This was Longfellow's first public support of abolitionism. However, as Longfellow himself said, the poems were "so mild that even a Slaveholder might read them without losing his appetite for breakfast". The New England Anti-Slavery Association, however, was satisfied enough with the intent of the collection to reprint it for their own distribution.

On May 10th, 1843, after seven years in pursuit, Longfellow received a letter from Fanny Appleton agreeing to marry him. He was elated and immediately walked 90 minutes to meet her at her house.

Nathan Appleton bought the Craigie House as a wedding present to the pair. Longfellow lived there for the rest of his life. His love for Fanny is evident from Longfellow's only love poem, the sonnet "The Evening Star", written in October 1845:

"O my beloved, my sweet Hesperus!
My morning and my evening star of love!"

He once attended a ball without her and said, "The lights seemed dimmer, the music sadder, the flowers fewer, and the women less fair."

Longfellow and Fanny had six children: Charles Appleton (1844), Ernest Wadsworth (1845), Fanny (1847, who died in infancy), Alice Mary (1850), Edith (1853), and Anne Allegra (1855).

Aware of his growing stature and his ability to influence others he also encouraged and supported many other translators. In 1845, he published The Poets and Poetry of Europe, a large 800-page compendium of translated works by other writers. Longfellow intended the anthology "to bring together, into a compact and convenient form, as large an amount as possible of those English translations which are scattered through many volumes, and are not accessible to the general reader".

On November 1st, 1847, the epic poem Evangeline was published.

Longfellow's literary income was now becoming quite substantial: in 1840, he had made $219 but by 1850 it had grown to a very promising $1,900.

On June 14th, 1853, Longfellow held a farewell dinner party at his Cambridge home for his great friend Nathaniel Hawthorne, who was preparing to move overseas.

In 1854, Longfellow retired from Harvard, devoting himself entirely to writing. He would be awarded an honorary doctorate of laws from Harvard in 1859.

The Song of Haiwatha, his epic poem, and perhaps his best known and enjoyed work was published in 1855.

On a hot July 9th day, 1861, Fanny was putting several locks of her children's hair into an envelope and making attempts to seal it with hot sealing wax while Longfellow took a nap. The circumstances of what happened next vary but the actuality is that Fanny's dress caught fire. Her screams awakened Longfellow who rushed to help her and threw a rug over her and stifled the flames with his own body as best he could, but Fanny was already horrifically burned.

A doctor was called and Fanny was taken to her room to recover. She was in and out of consciousness throughout the night and was also administered ether. The next morning, July 10th, 1861, she died shortly after 10 o'clock after asking for a cup of coffee.

Longfellow, in his effort to save her had also been badly burned and was unable to attend her funeral. His facial injuries required he stopped shaving. The ensuing beard now became the quintessential look that everyone remembers from pictures.

Devastated, he never fully recovered and sometimes resorted to laudanum and ether to ease the pain. He worried he would go insane and begged "not to be sent to an asylum" and noted that he was "inwardly bleeding to death". In the sonnet "The Cross of Snow" (1879), which he wrote eighteen years later he wrote:

"Such is the cross I wear upon my breast
These eighteen years, through all the changing scenes
And seasons, changeless since the day she died".

Longfellow spent several years translating Dante Alighieri's epic poem, The Divine Comedy. To aid him in perfecting the translation and reviewing proofs, he invited several friends to weekly meetings every Wednesday from 1864. This became known as the "Dante Club", and regulars included William Dean Howells, James Russell Lowell, Charles Eliot Norton and other occasional guests. The full three-volume translation was published in the spring of 1867, though Longfellow would continue to revise it. It was wildly popular and was re-printed four times in its first year.

By 1868, Longfellow's annual income was over a staggering $48,000.

Longfellow was also part of a group of Poets who became known as The Fireside Poets. The group included Longfellow, William Cullen Bryant, John Greenleaf Whittier, James Russell Lowell, and Oliver Wendell Holmes Snr. Occasionally Ralph Waldo Emerson is also placed among their number. The name "Fireside Poets" derives from poetry reading as a collective family entertainment of the times.

During the 1860s, Longfellow, still a committed abolitionist, also hoped for a coming together, a reconciliation, between the north and south after the dark days of the Civil War. When his son was wounded during the war, he wrote the poem "Christmas Bells", later the basis of the carol I Heard the Bells on Christmas Day.

In 1874, Samuel Cutler Ward helped him sell the poem "The Hanging of the Crane" to the New York Ledger for $3,000; it was the highest price ever paid for a poem. An astonishing sum. But Longfellow was worth it. His fame and audience were widespread and devoted.

Continuing in his hopes for a better and more united America he wrote in his journal in 1878: "I have only one desire; and that is for harmony, and a frank and honest understanding between North and South". Longfellow, despite his aversion to public speaking, took up an offer from Joshua Chamberlain to speak at his fiftieth reunion at Bowdoin College. Here he read the poem "Morituri Salutamus" so quietly that few could hear.

On August 22th, 1879, a female admirer who seemed to know little about his history, traveled to Longfellow's house in Cambridge and, unaware to whom she was speaking, asked Longfellow: "Is this the house where Longfellow was born?" Longfellow told her it was not. The visitor then asked if he had died here. "Not yet", he replied.

Much of Longfellow's work is recognized for its melody-like musicality. As he says, "what a writer asks of his reader is not so much to like as to listen".

Longfellow, like many others of the period, called for the development of high quality American literature. In his work, Kavanagh, a character says: "We want a national literature commensurate with our mountains and rivers... We want a national epic that shall correspond to the size of the country... We want a national drama in which scope shall be given to our gigantic ideas and to the unparalleled activity of our people... In a word, we want a national literature altogether shaggy and unshorn, that shall shake the earth, like a herd of buffaloes thundering over the prairies."

As a translator Longfellow was very impressive. His translation of Dante's The Divine Comedy became a requirement for those who wanted to be a part of high culture.

In 1874, Longfellow oversaw a 31-volume anthology called Poems of Places, collecting poems of several geographical locations; Europe, Asia, and the Arabian countries. It was a work of great educational endeavor but Emerson was disappointed and is said to have told Longfellow: "The world is expecting better things of you than this... You are wasting time that should be bestowed upon original production".

At this point in his life Longfellow could look back and see that his early collections, Voices of the Night and Ballads and Other Poems, had made him instantly popular. The New-Yorker called him "one of the very few in our time who has successfully aimed in putting poetry to its best and sweetest uses". The Southern Literary Messenger immediately put Longfellow "among the first of our American poets".

The rapidity with which American readers embraced Longfellow was unparalleled in publishing history in the United States. His popularity spread throughout Europe, his poems translated into Italian, French, German, and other languages.

Longfellow was the most popular poet of his day. As a friend once wrote to him, "no other poet was so fully recognized in his lifetime". Some of his works including "Paul Revere's Ride" and "The Song of Haiwatha" may have rewritten the facts but became essential parts of the American psyche and culture. He was so admired that on his 70th birthday in 1877 the atmosphere was that of a national holiday, with parades, speeches, and, of course, the reading of his poems.

Over the years, Longfellow's reputation came to include his personality; he was a gentle, placid, poetic soul. James Russell Lowell said, Longfellow had an "absolute sweetness, simplicity, and modesty". The reality was that Longfellow's life was much more difficult than was assumed. He suffered from neuralgia, which caused him constant pain, and poor eyesight. The difficulties of coping with the loss of two wives also took its toll. He was very quiet, reserved, and private; in later years, he became increasingly unsocial and avoided leaving home if he could.

In March 1882, Longfellow went to bed with severe stomach pain. He endured the pain for several days with the help of opium.

Henry Wadsworth Longfellow died, surrounded by family, on Friday, March 24th, 1882. He had been suffering from peritonitis.

He is buried with both of his wives at Mount Auburn Cemetery in Cambridge, Massachusetts. At Longfellow's funeral, his friend Ralph Waldo Emerson called him "a sweet and beautiful soul".

At the time of his death, his estate was valued at $356,320.

In 1884, Longfellow became the first non-British writer for whom a sculpted bust was placed in Poet's Corner of Westminster Abbey in London; he remains the sole American poet thus represented.

Henry Wadsworth Longfellow – A Concise Bibliography

Outre-Mer: A Pilgrimage Beyond the Sea (Travelogue) (1835)
Hyperion, a Romance (1839)
The Spanish Student. A Play in Three Acts (1843)
Evangeline: A Tale of Acadie (poem) (1847)
Kavanagh (1849)
The Golden Legend (poem) (1851)
The Song of Hiawatha (poem) (1855)
The New England Tragedies (1868)
The Divine Tragedy (1871)
Christus: A Mystery (1872)
Aftermath (poem) (1873)
The Arrow and the Song (poem)

Poetry Collections

Voices of the Night (1839)
Ballads & Other Poems (1841)
Poems on Slavery (1842)
The Belfry of Bruges & Other Poems (1845)
The Seaside and the Fireside (1850)
The Poetical Works of Henry Wadsworth Longfellow (1852)
The Courtship of Miles Standish & Other Poems (1858)
Tales of a Wayside Inn (1863)
Birds of Passage (1863)
Household Poems (1865)
Flower-de-Luce (1867)
Three Books of Song (1872)
The Masque of Pandora & Other Poems (1875)
Kéramos & Other Poems (1878)
Ultima Thule (1880)
In the Harbor (1882)

Michel Angelo: A Fragment (incomplete; published posthumously)